Gather Me Together, Lord

AND OTHER PRAYERS
FOR MOTHERS

Gather Me Together, Lord

AND OTHER PRAYERS FOR MOTHERS

Margaret B. Spiess

BAKER BOOK HOUSE

Grand Rapids, Michigan 49506

To

Marvin

without whom there
would be no book

Thanks to Mary Frances Carruth
for advice and encouragement,
and to Carol Seebach and Joyce
Rickwartz for clerical skills.

ISBN: 0-8010-8229-3

First printing, December 1982
Second printing, July 1983
Third printing, March 1984

Printed in the United States of America

Gather Me Together

Gather me together, Lord,
please gather me together!

This day was so hectic I feel like I've left
    bits and pieces of me
scattered all over.
There were the demands of the telephone
the doorbell
the family rushing off in different
    directions,
each with a special deadline,
and we even ate in relays.

And now this meeting
where I must appear calm
at ease
serene.
(Even this prayer was interrupted, Lord).

Show me how to order my life
to cope with days like these
or, better still, avoid them.
Calm me as my soul
    catches up with my body. . . .
Thank you for these quiet seconds
and for putting me back together.

Lord, If You Were a Housewife

Lord, if you were a housewife
your house would be orderly,
smell fragrant,
look inviting
and restful.
So how is it mine doesn't meet
even *one* of those standards
with regularity?
My house only looks lived-in!
If I wash the windows, I leave the ironing;
if I attend a meeting, the dishes go undone.
And when I'm vigorous and energetic
there's a score of interruptions.
I need help!

To keep our peace of mind psychiatrists say
we should do what seems necessary
get it done
and enjoy it.

Give me good judgment
about my work.
Help me put things away
not just down
and let me enjoy my job.

Common Things

Open me to joy, Lord,
to the lilting rhythm of life!
Let me be aware of the loveliness
    of common things:
sunlight on a crisp autumn morning
the soft sweet scent of four-o'clocks
our dog's trusting eyes;
the rhythmic roar of the ocean
a smile on the face of a friend
the tinkle of laughter;
a dearly loved voice, singing in the shower
the freshness of my body
    after a good night's sleep
dew sparkling on a rose petal
leaves crunching underfoot
the possibilities and plans
    you have for our world.
I'm glad I'm a part of it, Lord.
Thank you!

Lord, Who Owns
My Time?

Lord, who owns my time?
You?
The PTA?
My family?
Me?
The church?
I'm one of the "nonworking" mothers
and so have quantities of time.
Where, Lord, *where*?
I want to respond to need,
but where is the cut-off point?
Must I contribute my time to a project
   I lack faith in?
To something I consider busy-work?
To tasks unworthy of intelligent women?
(Don't they consider
   their time worth more, too?)
And yet if I refuse, I'm haunted by guilt.

You gave each of us a special task, Lord.
I must not neglect mine:
to attend a meeting
   just because "it's time" for one
or to make potholders to sell to feed the
   poor!

I'm jealous of my time, Lord,
(more than my money,
    which I have less of).
Let me use time wisely
and please, show me how to say no
    to unreasonable demands on it.

Luncheon

I didn't want to attend this luncheon, Lord.
There were so many other things to do.
It was just going to be
    another surface touching,
I thought,
no real involvement.
But there was true friendship there today,
    Lord,
real sharing
and I felt warmed as I left.
Thank you
    for sending me out to lunch today.

All That Counts

We're together again, Lord, all of us —
here and vibrant and alive!
Thank you!
We've had some narrow
  escapes these last years, Lord,
but we're here now
and unharmed!
We should be singing your praises
  every minute.
We, who have felt your hand
and your abiding presence
in the darkest hours,
should be praying without ceasing
for those in distress
  and pain and sorrow now,
for those who don't know
  they can turn to you . . .
and we should thank you for giving us
  another chance.
But we get busy, Lord,
rushing here and there
doing household chores
complaining about the weather
fussing because we haven't enough time.
Lord, we *have* the time.

We know
    none of these things really matter.
All that counts is that we're together and
    you're here
with us
loving us
always.

Many Voices

You must have a great sense of humor,
    Lord,
or you'd be outraged at these songs
they sing about you.
They're not orthodox
or even kosher,
but remind me that there are
    many ways to seek you
and many voices through which you speak.

Seventy Times Seven

Unto seventy times seven, Lord?
Forgive that many times . . .
and more?
Forgive so completely the offense is blotted
    out of mind?
I can't!
Lord, help me,
for I can't!
Little things keep reminding me
and I hurt all over again
as if the wound were new.

I *want* to forgive,
to restore this relationship
that was very precious to me.
My heart aches with this agony.
Help me.
Forgive me my unforgiving heart.

But, Lord,
    which is more important to me—
my pride and disillusionment
or this friendship?
Lord, is just wanting to forgive a start?
I *do* want to

with all my heart!
Help me
and help her,
the unforgiving
and the unforgiven.

I have no right to talk with you
until my heart is right again,
but, Lord,
don't turn your back on me,
please.
Give me faith and hope again.
Absolve us both from our guilt.
You who died for the sins of the world,
did you die for my unyielding heart?

Oh, Lord, forgive me as I forgive her.
Help me handle
    the reminders of this ordeal with love.
Alone I cannot do it
but "I can do all things through Christ
    which strengtheneth me."*
Grant me your strength.

*Philippians 4:13

His Praise Shall Continually Be in My Mouth

"His praise shall continually be
   in my mouth."*
Continually?
Does that mean I should praise you
even when I don't want to,
when praise seems
(excuse me, Lord)
unmerited
or out of place?

Sometimes
   praising God
   seems more than I can do!

I don't feel full of praise
when the dentist is drilling
or the children are fighting
or the doctor is probing;
when there's been an accident
or the washer overflows
or my head is pounding. . . .

*Psalm 34:1

Screaming? Yes.
Crying? Maybe.
But *praising*?

But are those the very times I *should*
 praise you?
Would praise put the incident in perspective
and free my mind to hear you speak?

Don't let me wait until I understand. . . .
Just help me praise now
and learn later.

Balance

I'm glad there's balance in your plan, Lord.
That for pain there is relief,
for sorrow comfort,
that nothing is enduring
except the greatest gift of all,
your love!

Sometimes It's Hard Not to "Play God"

Sometimes it's hard not to "play God,"
  Lord,
really hard!
When I see someone I love struggling
  with a problem
and I think I see the solution he cannot see
I want to help.

But I have tunnel vision
  where my loved one is concerned.

It's almost more than I can bear
  to stand aside,
hands off and mouth shut,
while he suffers.

Give me wisdom.
Help me *want* to be quiet and prayerful
and to leave the solution to you.

Lord, Do We Sometimes Hamper You?

Lord, do we sometimes hamper you
   by giving up too soon;
by picturing the accident or illness
in all its gory detail while praying;
forgetting you're within
and around
and above the patient
waiting to release your vitality
waiting for your healing to be accepted?
We take the illness as ultimate reality
when you and your loving power
are the overriding truth.

We pray, Lord;
teach us how!

Not Quite Well

When did this happen, Lord?

When did I start thinking about myself
    as being
not sick
but not quite well?
When did I join the women
    who compare operations
and give "organ recitals"
    at the hint of a headache?
"How many stitches?"
"Did you have X rays?"
"The doctor never saw such a bad case!"

How tiresome!
Can it be that I'm encouraging
    my not-quite-wellness?

Let me limit discussions of my viscera
to my doctor
and give me more interesting things
    to talk about.

Thank you for my body
and its wellness.

I Want to Cry

There's something wrong with me;
the doctors confirm it.
I want to cry, Lord,
just cry . . . and cry . . . and cry
until I am utterly spent.
Sick? Me?
Oh, sure, I've felt a twinge here and there
but I'm the healthy one.
I'm the woman with all the energy
    to do everything.
Ride a bike, pound a typewriter,
    play tennis, jog, camp, hike—
Thank you, Lord, for that energy.
Thank you, that though I discovered
    my body and its vibrancy late,
it's served me well.

Could it keep on serving me,
serving me well,
a little longer?
No, I'll be honest:
Not a *little* longer but a *lot* longer.
Thank you for my body
    and its marvelous design.
Show me how to cooperate with you
in getting well.

Running Scared

Lately I'm always running scared, Lord.
Where is my faith?

I fear for my loved ones
when they're out of my sight
(as if I could protect them!).

I'm afraid of auto accidents
illness
arguments
old age
loneliness
estrangement
atomic disaster
war
race riots
the drug culture!

"Just in case," I worry in advance.
I'm apprehensive today
for next week
next month
next year.
It's hurting me and distressing my family.
Help me
    to stop worrying.
Show me

how to feel your presence
to launch out in faith
to be calm
and quiet
and trusting.

Renew My Mind

The doctors don't know
    what's wrong with me;
they shake their heads and look grave.
I'm puzzled, too, Lord,
but this I do know:
You can heal me
if I ask, *believing*,
and if I get out of my own way!
First I must try to correct my mind.

"Be ye transformed by the
    renewing of your mind."
"Let this mind be in you,
    which was also in Christ Jesus. . . ."*

Jesus' mind in mine?
Lord, take my mind and make it yours.
Show me the way to wholeness and health.

*Romans 12:2; Philippians 2:5

My Heart Is Leaden, Lord

My heart is leaden, Lord,
and my head brought low.
Every fiber of my being
   aches with my distress.
It's as though you weren't in your heaven
or here
or anywhere!

Where are you, Lord?

I can neither see nor hear you!
I am lost
alone
adrift
and desolate.
Help me, Lord!
Mayday! Mayday!

I want to cry
(as I did all night)
to scream
to rant
to destroy those who wounded me!

And yet you, Lord,
are within the very hearts
of those who hurt me!
Why do they have such power over me?

There must be something salvageable
some hope
some lesson to be learned. . . .
Show me
and be patient with me
when I'm slow to understand.

Replace My Thoughts

Lord, I can't take these negative thoughts
that are trying to possess me!
I reject them.
But, quick, I must have
   something to replace them
or they'll rush back,
greatly multiplied,
into the void.

"In quietness and in confidence
shall be your strength."*

Help me
as I try to be quiet
to be confident
to be strong.

* Isaiah 30:15

Defrosting Time

It's defrosting time again, Lord,
and I must face it:
I waste food!
So far I've managed to conceal this fault
from my family,
but *you* know
and I know
and I'm ashamed.

The celery I bring home from the market
crisp, green, and inviting
bears almost no resemblance
   to that hiding in the crisper
slimy and brown.
These moldy oranges,
that hairy rice
bear witness to this sin.
Do we have too much?
Are we spoiled?

No matter how I try
there's always something left over:
fifteen beans
half of a deviled egg
a quarter of a sandwich
a withered apple.

I must decide:
Shall I throw it out now
or wait till it grows whiskers?
Almost never can I
gauge appetites accurately.

"A woman can throw out more
with a spoon
than a man can bring in with a shovel."
If I'd used that half loaf of bread
or stored it in the freezer
rather than letting it mold
I'd have fifty cents more
for the offering plate.
With what I waste I might feed
a starving child.

Let me see food through your eyes —
as a gift of your bounty.
Help me be thrifty
and attentive to potential waste.
Correct my sense of timing
so I'll use food at its peak.
And let no one suffer
because of my wastefulness.

Second Thought

It is wrong, Lord, for me to pray,
asking that you make someone better
or kinder
or more tractable
to make her easier for me to love!

That's unfair!

I'm loved, Lord.
In spite of my faults and unreasonableness
I am loved.

Thank you for my friends and family
who didn't wait until I became perfect
(they'd be waiting till the last trump!)
or easy to get along with
before they loved me.

Why can't I be at least as generous
   with my love as they?
Help me to be patient.
Let me show loving-kindness.
Habitually,
and not just
   when everyone is behaving well!

Let Me Show Love

You show me daily that you love me, Lord;
does my family deserve any less from me?
Help me to demonstrate
in unmistakable ways
that I love them individually.

Some days one needs me
    more than the others,
but they all need to know,
each of them,
every day,
that I love them
as we know you love us all.

In the Slough of Despond

If I were to list my blessings,
I'd have to start 'way back
   before I was born
and it would take a long time —
   maybe forever.
So what am I doing slogging around,
like Christian in the Slough of Despond?
I've been mired here for days, weeks even,
and I can't seem to get out.
What's the matter with me, Lord?
Of course I have my troubles
but I haven't seen anyone with a better set
so that I'd want to exchange with him!

If this depression is physical,
   show me what to do.
If it's mental, or a combination of the two,
   direct me.
And if it's plain old cussedness, Lord,
hold up a mirror and let me see myself
(but may I see
   your loving-kindness mirrored there, too?).

Grant me perspective
and a sense of humor
and a long, strong rope
to haul myself out of this valley of despair.

Why Does Forgiving Come So Hard to Me?

Why does forgiving come so hard to me,
   Lord?
Before I grant pardon do I
want to be sure the other person
understands perfectly
how much she's hurt me?
Is it because I want her to suffer
the agony she's made me feel?
Do I want her to grovel?

I'm confused
embarrassed
and ashamed
to see this sin revealed,
raw and coarse and ugly.
I can hardly believe this of myself!

Show me how to change,
teach me to forgive
as I would like to be forgiven.

Dishes and Dust Curls

Lord, didn't I wash these same dishes
  yesterday?
Make the same beds?
Scrub the same floor?
Rout the same dust?
Launder the same clothes?
How can I ever catch up?
Even when I prepare a great meal,
we need feeding again a short while later.
Nothing *stays* done, Lord!
Nothing ever stays neat
or clean
or finished. . . .
And no one ever stays fed!
No wonder housewifery
  has such a bad name!

But, Lord,
   you do the same things every day,
bringing the sun up,
placing the clouds,
darkening the sky at evening . . .
yet *your* work is done with such a flair
as to delight the heart!
My tasks are humble, Lord,
but necessary.
Let me do them graciously
with loving-kindness and good humor.
And please, Lord,
teach me to deal creatively
with dishes
and dust curls!

Today

I'm about to climb the walls, Lord!
My thoughts are whirling
dredging up yesterday's troubles
anticipating tomorrow's.

But today is new, Lord!
This bright, shining day
is a gift from you.
There is no reason
why it can't be radiant and lovely
in memory tomorrow
if I seek and follow your guidance
today.

Direct my thoughts
guide my words
instruct my hands
and lead me through this day
so when I return it to you tonight
it shall be
as flawless
as when you gave it.

Mountaintop

It was great, Lord,
really great!
The view from the mountain magnificent
(you remember!)
and as I related the experience
I wanted everyone to feel as I did
but their expressions said
"Really?"
or
"How nice!"
and my memory began to falter.
Was it truly wonderful?
Were you really there?
Was I?

Dear Lord, don't let the vision fade!
Guard this warm spot in my heart.
Let me keep it
as a buffer against loneliness,
reassurance for a time of anguish.

The Times in Between

I'm grateful, Lord, for this time in between.
We are all well.
We've no pressing problems
there's no rush today
no pressure
    forcing me into a state of tension
not even anyone I'm worried about.
Thank you, Lord!

Sometimes I feel I couldn't make it
without the times in between.
And yet I know you're always with me
through the quiet times
the glad times
days of sorrow
hours of frustration. . . .
"My Lord knows the way
    through the wilderness,
all I have to do is follow"
says a children's chorus.
Thank you
    for the promise of your presence
and for making this a calm and restful
in-between day.

On the Beam

New ideas
   are bombarding me from all directions
new ways of eating
new ways of learning
new ways of healing
space exploration
UFOs
the psychic world . . .
what is the truth?

Lord, don't let me reject an idea
just because it's new
and jostles my beliefs.
Let me put it to the test.
You're older than the hills
yet as modern as day after tomorrow
and may be trying to show me something.

Sometimes I need stirring up.
Show me the way
and keep me
   safely on the beam of your love.

Ask!

Lord, you really mean it!
*"Ask, and ye shall receive."**

Ask
wholeheartedly
singlemindedly
without looking back
taking my eyes off the "real" condition
and looking steadfastly
   into your shining face. . . .

Ask
believing with all of my being
heart
mind
soul
body. . . .

Ask
with patience
and faith unwavering. . . .

Ask
in your name
with prayer
and thanksgiving. . . .

"Ask,
and ye *shall* receive!"

*John 16:24

You Must Love Us Very Much, Lord

You must love us very much, Lord,
to make our world so beautiful!
If man had created the sun,
it would burn more often than it warmed
and when it rose and set
it would be like flipping a light switch.
But you made even the rising
   and setting of the sun exquisite,
bracketing each day
   with proof of your love.

You gave us fleecy clouds, Lord,
and bright autumn leaves,
wild wind
silvery rain
emerald trees
and springing grass!
Glowing moonlight
rainbows
mountain shadows
and soft warm earth. . . .
My heart aches with the splendor of it all.

O Lord,
   let me not squander your prodigal gifts!

Resist Not

"Resist not evil. . . ."
". . . but overcome evil with good."*
Resist not?
But I want to fight
to conquer this force
    that seems bent on felling me.
**All that energy and attention
    strengthen the wrong.**
But how can I sit back
    and ignore the situation?
What situation?
Why, the one I see,
the real facts of the case.
**Are you sure
    you have 20–20 vision in this matter?
Do you see with the eyes of Christ?
Analyze with the mind of Christ?**
W-e-l-l, no, . . .
**How far have you gotten
living your way?**
Not anywhere, Lord,
just round and round a maze,
the matter worsening all the while.

*Matthew 5:39a; Romans 12:21b

Would you care to try a better way?
Yes, Lord, but I'm afraid.
Fear not.
I am with you wherever you go.
It seems so passive
so surrendering. . . .
Have you a better plan?
No plan at all
I'm at the end of my tether
and desperate.
Are you willing to let it all go?
To give the entire problem to me
with no thought of the why
or the how
or even the when
of its solution?
That's a large order, Lord.
What if I forget . . .
I know I will at times . . .
and start to advise you?
I'll be prepared,
I'll help you turn your thoughts to me.
Then there won't be room
   for worry or fear.
You think we can do it, Lord?
I'm willing.
Okay, Lord, I'll take the plunge —
just stay close by.
I need you so.

Joy Cometh
in the Morning

Thank you, Lord, that though
   "weeping may endure for a night, . . .
joy cometh in the morning."*

I've felt trapped,
boxed in
with no light visible,
no way out of the maze,
almost unable to pray.

Yet here I am
relaxed
relieved
restored
and I cannot say when or how
   you released me!

Thank you, Lord,
thank you!

Help me to remember
next time
this, too, shall pass,
you're in your heaven
(and on earth in the hearts of men)
and all can be right
   with my world once again.

*Psalm 30:5

Cartwheels

Today I feel young
and lithe
and eager!
Like turning cartwheels down the street
or running barefoot through a meadow
or hugging everyone I see!
It's as though I were seventeen again,
only better!
Thank you, Lord.

I don't know where the bubbly feeling
  came from
but, as I crossed the street,
it was as if you said,
"I love you,"
using *my* name,
and suddenly I heard and believed you!

I used to have these shout-for-joy times
often
as a child
but even then they came unheralded.
Let my soul be childlike again, Lord,
open and free and receptive
to these delightful evidences of your love.

Thank you,
O thank you!

Impasse

I've reached an impasse, Lord.
Let me relax and give the situation over
into your hands.

Take it, Lord;
I relinquish my hold on it.
Bless this problem,
its solution,
and those involved in it,
that we all may
"let go
    and let God have his wonderful way."

And throughout the day,
as my mind returns to it
(I am only human, Lord),
help me feel a tangible sense
    of your hand in mine
your thoughts in my thoughts
your love in my heart.

Self-image

I need help with my self-image, Lord!
I'm constantly discounting myself.
I feel so inept —
only, to quote Lisa of "Green Acres,"
"I'm as ept as anyone!"

I need a sense of accomplishment each day.
Encourage me
and when necessary
let me be my own cheering squad.

I Try, Lord

I try, Lord,
I really do try to be a good mother!
(Maybe I try too hard?)
I must learn to give help
only when asked,
and not assume
   I always know what's needed.
Things change so fast
I need a barometer to gauge moods
or a scorecard
   to identify the players and their positions!
Let me be perceptive.
I want to uphold,
not nag, my children.

I'm often inflexible
when I need to be adaptable, Lord.
I must allow them
   to make their own mistakes
and learn from them.
My trouble is
I love not wisely
but too well.

I wonder
now and then
why I ever applied for the job!
(Yet I wouldn't have it otherwise.)

Guard my relationship
   with each of my children, Lord.
Sometimes it's a fragile, tenuous thing.
Give them patience with me.
When I'm tired
or angry
or hurt,
control my tone of voice
my words
and even the furrows in my brow, Lord,
so they can detect
beyond and underneath the scolding
the true love I bear them.

And help me, Lord,
to hold those I love
in an open hand.

Needed

I want to be useful, Lord,
to be needed.
And I am needed now.

Oh, mostly they don't realize it,
    but they do need me, Lord,
don't they?

Let me be needed
    and let me meet their needs.

Right now the need is mine, Lord.
I need to feel loved,
to be cuddled.
If my mother were here, I'd sit on her lap!
But she's gone and I'm a grown woman.
I'm supposed to be strong, as she was.
Thank you for her example
and for being needed.

Back in the Fold

Here I am again, Lord!
I'm back — back in the fold.
After I've been gone so long.

Oh, I didn't forget you
but there were so many things to do
so much activity
so much care
that we didn't get together
as often as we should have.

Thank you for waiting for me
loving me
protecting me
even when I forget you!

Strangers

They took us in, Lord!
We were strangers, in a wreck
and far from home,
and they took us in.
They ministered unto us,
bringing fragrant blooms
   from their gardens —
colorful sweet peas,
shaggy bachelor buttons,
yellow daisies.
They offered transportation,
sent cards,
picked succulent raspberries and
luscious apricots for us
whom they had never seen before.

And they prayed. . . .
They prayed, Lord, for us!
And their prayers were in their ministering.
They performed their duties
   with compassion
and love
and laughter.

Thank you, especially,
    for those who made us laugh!
The accident
    that could have been a nightmare
became bearable
with their love.
In time that's all we'll remember . . .
not the pain or the worry or the fear
but your love
    that surrounded us in the form
of those nurses at Faith Hospital.

Bless them, Lord,
    and those they minister unto today.
Thank you that there are those
who are kind
    to the strangers within their gates.

And help us to be more openhanded,
more free in showing love to all we meet,
less afraid to be friendly,
for freely we have received
and should surely freely give.

Gimme Girl

I'm getting to be a regular "gimme girl,"
   Lord.
I'm continually asking for something,
wheedling,
   like a small child who wants a cookie
or a dog who smells fresh meat.

Is that the way you operate, Lord?
Do we have to bombard heaven
   with our repetitions?
Thank you for not being deaf
and for being infinitely patient.

Thank you, Lord,
   for the many times you've stood by
and held my hand
for the glad times I've had
for the love I've known.

And with your help,
   perhaps I can even be thankful
for this present problem,
knowing you see the way through
and you're helping all of us.

Lovest Thou Me?

"Lovest thou me?
Lovest thou me more than these?"*
To be honest, Lord
(and I cannot be otherwise with you,
although I've tried),
if you ask me this
I'll have to say, "I don't know!"
Love you more than husband
children
parents
when I sometimes ache with love for them?
And yet it is *you in them*
    that makes them lovable
for you are love.
Could I love you through them?
But there are others you want me to love
who are not so lovely. . . .

Inasmuch as ye do it unto the least —
the most unlovable —
of these. . . .
"Lovest thou me?"

*John 21:15 – 17

Eye of the Hurricane

Goodness! How glad I am
   that you're not emotional, Lord!
I'm fed up with people with bruised egos
hurt feelings
quick tempers
bad moods
melancholia.

It's great that I can talk with you
and know that nothing I say or do
or leave unsaid or undone
will cause you to bang doors
or retire to a corner of heaven and sulk!

Thank you for being dependable
steady
strong
and *calm*.

Through the Eyes of Love

Not the sags, the bags, and the wrinkles,
  Lord,
don't let him notice them!
Oh, I'm not asking to appear eighteen
  again
(that would be a miracle
and I couldn't keep up the illusion),
but please don't let him see me
  as I see myself,
with merciless clarity.

He deserves a winsome wife —
neat, trim, and comely.
Help me be my best for him.

And please
let him see me always
through the eyes of love.

No Favorites, Lord!

No favorites, Lord!
Please, let me have no favorites!
The youngest child thinks
   I love the oldest best;
the middle thinks I champion the youngest;
the oldest is sure the middle child is my pet.
The girls think I favor the boy.
He thinks the girls come first.
Help!
I love them all.

Of the eldest I thought for a long time,
will I ever understand this child?
But now we're friends
and I can't recall the problem.
It's bound to be so with the others,
isn't it?

Lord, I love each of my children,
desperately and often selfishly,
but I can't love them all the same way!
They respond differently.

What to one is delightful
is annoying to another.
Each is a distinct individual,
exasperating
complex
and endearing,
and I'm glad.
But I am only one
and must learn with each of them.
Show me how to respond
   to each child's need
in the manner most acceptable to him
to convince him he's special and very dear.
I'm so proud of my children
I'm sometimes embarrassed
by my unrestrained glowing.

Help me, Lord, to win them over,
away from jealousy.
Thank you for my children.

Now

Thank you, Lord, for *now*.
This time in history
this day
this hour
this minute!

Thank you for life today
perplexing
challenging
disturbing
mind-bending in its possibilities.

Show me how to live it
use it
glorify it
so that because of me
living here and now,
fully aware,
your kingdom will come a little nearer
a little sooner

I Can Read, Lord!

I can read, Lord!
I can *read*!
Since I've been doing it
   longer than I'd care to mention,
this is no surprise to you . . .
but I've never thanked you
   for this special joy!

Thank you, Lord,
for writers who can stir me
move me to tears
double me up with laughter
stretch my mind
set my soul glowing.
Thank you, Lord!
Let me use this gift well.

Fit for a King

Everything
   went together beautifully tonight,
   Lord,
and the dinner was fit for a king,
or company, at least.
Although no one mentioned it
I know the meal was enjoyed.
The aromas were mouth-watering,
the colors inviting,
the foods contrasted in texture
and tasted great.
When a meal turns out this way,
cooking is fun.

Thank you for times
like tonight
when routine wears a ruffle.

Late Supper

We were all cross tonight, Lord,
touchy and irritated,
some at the point of tears—
I wondered why
and then I looked at the clock.
Supper was at least an hour late.

Help me remember that people
(as well as the dog and the cat)
become cross when hungry.

And please help me keep track of the hours
and serve supper on time.

Sometimes
I *Can't* Pray,
Lord!

Sometimes I *can't* pray, Lord!
Black despair covers everything
so I can't even think of you,
only how I failed.
I berate myself with tortured questions:
Why hadn't I done this differently?
Or that earlier?

When I come to,
sometimes days later,
and try to pray
my words hit the ceiling and bounce back
hard and cold
like so much hail.
It's terrifying!

At such times remind me, Lord,
that you don't require proof
   of good behavior

before you deign to hear my prayers.
Perhaps, when I'm so muddled,
   I pray amiss.
Maybe just your name
a receptive heart
and a listening mind
would suffice.

Reassure me, Lord,
   so I'll know with my mind
and accept deep within my heart
your promise that nothing can separate me
   from your love . . .
nothing.

Anniversary

Thank you, Lord, for my husband,
this man who has put up with me
and loved me
for twenty-five years.
(That's a quarter of a century, Lord!
Not long to you, of course,
but more than a third
    of a man's alloted lifetime.)
And yet it seems so short.

He's more handsome than when we
    married;
I like his graying hair
and his strong, supple body.

He's more interesting, too,
with a quick, active mind.

Thank you for his patience
when I was overwrought and angry
(more times than I like to remember).
Though he says little about it,

I know he loves me
and always has.

Oh, he's no saint, Lord,
thank goodness!
I couldn't have stood
  being married to a man
who was a doormat
or sickeningly sweet.
Thank you for the spice of our arguments
and most of all
though we are one
  in all the important ways,
that we're each still complete individuals,
more complete and individual
than if we'd remained single!

Bless our marriage, Lord,
strengthen it as our children leave home
and please give us
  many more productive years together,
my beloved and me.

Comfort My Friend

What about my friend, Lord,
what can I do for her?
With her husband's death
    she lost part of herself.
He was one of your special ones, Lord.
(They used to call them "saints"
but he would have laughed to hear
    such a term applied to him.)

They were both "prepared" for this parting
but, Lord, how could they be . . .
they who loved each other so dearly?
They were married so long
she can scarcely recall being single!

Comfort her
    in the lonely stretches of the night.
Lord, bless her in her grief.
Let her express it wisely
(not bottle it up and become ill).
Keep her mind active
her body agile
and her spirit filled
    with the comforting presence
of your abiding love.

Burdens

"Everyone has his own proper burden[s]
    to bear."*
My own proper burdens?
With your help I'll carry them.
But save me from an Atlas complex,
from piously parading with a cross
    you never wanted me to have!

Many of us bear unnecessary burdens
dragging around heavy hearts
remembering some failure
cherishing a slight
repeating it to sympathetic ears with a sigh.

But, Lord, in dying for our sins,
did you include our unnecessary burdens?
Take mine, dear Lord;
I'm sick to death of them!

*Galatians 6:5, NEB

Drained

I feel drained, Lord,
utterly drained!
I've given all I can give,
more than I ever knew I had,
to this problem.
I have no more.
Take over, Lord.
I relinquish it to you.
(I should have done so long ago.)
Please take this tangled mass
and straighten it
so that the weaving can be straight
and smooth
and perfect,
according to your plan.

A Very Present Friend

Thank you for sharing my life, Lord,
for being interested in my concerns.
I'm glad I can talk with you
while I make the beds,
burn the toast,
hang the clothes,
or cut my finger.
You showed me that "thee" is not
  necessary,
or kneeling required.
Just being in your presence,
as with a friend,
is enough.

A Prayer for Harmony

I love my children, Lord,
and I want them to love each other.
They are great people
each quite different
but every one special
and very dear.

Help them to see each other as individuals,
as friends.
Show them each other's best qualities
and make them tolerant
   of the others' faults
and friends.
Give us harmony at home
and let us love each other
as you love us.

It's Easy to Kill a Child's Dream

It's easy to kill a child's dream, Lord!
All it takes is a thoughtless remark.
"Don't you know that'll never work?"
"Wait and I'll show you
  how to do it right!"
"You were great, honey,
but why didn't you hold your head up?"
"Next time ask me first."

Our sense of wonder is lost all too soon.
We must not stifle theirs.

Bless my starry-eyed children, Lord.
Keep their visions bright.

Time to Let Go

It's time for me to let go now, Lord;
help me, for I don't want to.
They may be ready
but I'm not.

As my children leave home
to become what you planned them to be
I want to call them back.
"Wait! Did you change your socks?
Be sure to get enough sleep.
Remember to write!"
and all such motherly reminders
that filled their days and mine.

But surely, Lord,
    I taught them more than that!
I want them to be
    independent, unique individuals,
to fulfill their destinies,
but have I prepared them for life?

There's so much yet they must learn . . .
let me free them
    to make their own discoveries.
Let me care enough to let them go.
I can't follow them, Lord,
but will *you* please go along

to guide and protect them?
Bring them through trials and temptations
with a consciousness of your constant love.
VAYAN CON DIOS, MY CHILDREN!

Pillar of Salt

I'd make a dandy pillar of salt, Lord!
I'm always looking back.
Guard me from wanting
   to turn back the clock
to the "good old days."
I'm living *today*.
My duty
my challenge
my joy
is here in the now of life.
Let me live this day well.

Waiting

"Organize your day
schedule your activities
plan your work
and work your plan!"
Splendid! I'll try it!
So why am I waiting in the car
with my tasks undone at home?
I can feel my muscles tensing.
Can I get everything done in time?
This unscheduled errand was to take
"just a minute."
But the minutes add up.

So many interruptions, Lord!
How am I to cope with them?
No matter how closely planned,
my days always bring variations . . .
phone calls
visits (rare)
salesmen. . . .

Is there a purpose in these changes?
What is required of me
during the waiting hours . . .
in check-out lines
at the vet's
in the doctor's anterooms
or when the car won't start?
Bits
pieces
tag ends
fragments of time . . .
how should I use them?

Thank you, Lord, for time . . .
for any time at all
for all the time allotted me.
Let me use it well.

Show Me How to Keep My Mouth Shut!

I'm so opinionated, Lord!
There's scarcely anything on which I'm
   unwilling to express my views.
(And the less welcome they are,
   the more determined I am to speak!)
I seem to think that if you
   needed a holiday
I could handle things quite well myself!

Now, Lord, you know the statements
   I make with such authority
are only personal opinions
   warped by an all-too-narrow viewpoint.
You know there's nothing pontifical
   about my pronouncements!
But I persist in giving unsolicited advice!

Sometimes when I think of what I've said
(always *after* the damage is done)
I'm amazed at my temerity
   in expressing myself
on what was clearly none of my concern.
Why do people put up with me?

When I feel a gush of advice
   flooding to my lips,

rush me from the room
   before I alienate anyone
and show me, Lord,
   how to keep my mouth shut!

The Argument

When my loved ones argue seriously
I get cold and numb inside
remembering other families
who haven't spoken in years.

O Lord, help us with our difficulties,
show us our faults,
lead us to ask forgiveness
before it is too late.

Heal the rift, dear Lord,
and keep my family together
in love
always.

Make Me a Miser, Lord!

Everyone else is asleep after a long day
while I,
tired
cross
and unwilling,
am doing the dishes.
At this hour
throwing them out the window
has definite appeal!
Help me find some way to get through.

As I wash these dishes
let me wash my mind
    of the day's annoyances
disappointments
failures . . .
but the good times must not drain away.
Help me sort them out,
treasure them
like panning gold.

Instead of the cross salesgirl
let me remember my son's laughter;
instead of the missed appointment,
the letter from a friend.
Sometimes the nuggets are small,

the panning tedious,
but each day has gold for me to garner . . .
make me a miser, Lord!

Be Jubilant, My Feet

"Be jubilant, my feet!"*
How I'd love to have jubilant feet, Lord!
Mine are worrisome
weary
and woeful
not to mention aching
and swollen.
Make them jubilant, Lord,
jubilant feet!

*From "The Battle Hymn of the Republic"

A Pine Forest in My Heart

I asked for time alone,
a solitary retreat
to calm my soul
and rest my body . . .
A deserted beach?
I'd walk barefoot on wet sand
waves lapping at my toes
the rhythm of the sea a lullaby
my troubles ebbing with the tide . . .
but the sea is far away!

I asked for time alone . . .
the mountains, closer by?
I'd lie on a carpet of pine needles
listen to the wind sighing through the trees
and watch the clouds
or count the stars . . .
but that was not to be.

You gave me time alone
without the ocean
without the hills
only this busy parking lot
while I await my load.
But you gave me a hiding place within,
a secret corner where you dwell.
Furnish it with cool places
as I need them. . . .

Give me a pine forest in my heart!

Flexible and Fulfilled

I plan to do something creative . . .
write a good story
make a new dress
compose an unforgettable poem . . .
and what happens?
I find myself cleaning the refrigerator
(I was only looking for celery for the soup),
scrubbing the floor
(someone might come),
doing the ironing
(it can't wait),
and the day is over
the idea lost
the opportunity gone.
At day's end I have
    a poignant sense of loss.

Other times I ignore the clutter
and do something to satisfy my soul.
Then my duties pile up and I feel guilty.

I need to get organized
but each time I try
the day is riddled with interruptions.

Lord, show me how to be a good steward
    of my responsibilities
and talents.
Let me be flexible
and fulfilled.

Dearly Beloved

"Dearly beloved. . . ."
Lord, we are gathered here
to unite this man
and this woman
in holy matrimony.
Man? That child?
He's so young, Lord,
and so vulnerable!
Strengthen him for the responsibilities he
    faces.
Woman? Oh, no, just a girl!

But Lord, here they are,
on the threshold of the great adventure,
pledging their lives
and their love to each other.
Join their souls, Lord,
as well as their bodies,
that they may be truly one.
Let them remember to laugh
    when things get hard.
Let them grow in this marriage, Lord,
so each
in having the other
is enabled to become
more than he could have been alone.

Be a part of their life,
and please, Lord, let this marriage
of these special friends
become one of your best success stories.

Change

We sing "Change and decay
   in all around I see"
in the lovely old hymn,*
   but *must* change result in decay?
Can't it be change and challenge?
Change and renewal?
Change and growth?

Let me welcome change
or at least not cringe from it.
Let me see its possibilities.
I can't do this alone
for I'm rather fond of my own routine,
but please, Lord,
show me the potential
   in each change in my life.

*From "Abide with Me"

Today's My Birthday, Lord

Today's my birthday, Lord,
the start of my own personal new year.
Where have the hours gone?
What have I done with my time?
What have I learned?
Have I grown at all
in any way that counts?

Looking back I see things I wish I hadn't
    done
(or had done differently)
chances I missed
joys I didn't recognize.

Keep me from looking back with regret.
I've tried . . .

you know I've tried . . .
mostly in my own strength
when I should have relied on you . . .
but that's over now
and this day begins a new year,
an opportunity uniquely mine.
Thank you for this birthday,
for another whole year
   of your love and companionship.
Go with me now into my new year . . .
and please grant me other birthdays
when I might give a better accounting.

Rainbow
on My Kitchen Floor

There was a rainbow on my kitchen floor
    this morning
not miles away and unreachable
but close enough to touch
and my very own,
emerald and pink
gold and violet
iridescent
glowing
especially for me!

Now the sun has shifted,
the floor is neutral
serviceable
and drab again.
But I had my rainbow, Lord!
For a few minutes my kitchen was
    transformed
by that small disk of color,
enough to warm my heart
    for days to come.

You often prepare rainbows for me;
let me be "at home" to receive them.

Judge Not

The Indians say we should never
   judge a man
until we've walked a mile in his moccasins.
Help me remember that, Lord.

I haven't walked in the shoes of others
but I have criticized them
for their short tempers
their moodiness
their cynicism
their foul language.
But I haven't been there, Lord,
not where they live!

I don't know their families
or the pressures that weigh them down.

You know them and love them, Lord,
in spite of their faults . . .
and you love me
in spite of my self-righteousness!

Your ways are not my ways
or your thoughts my thoughts.
For this I am humbly grateful.

Could I Be Wrong, Lord?

Could I be wrong, Lord?
Could I possibly be wrong?
Oh, my record of being in error
I'd match with anyone . . .
but in *this*?
It's almost more than I can take!

Let me realize,
or to be more honest,
let me *want* to accept
that what's right for me in this
may not be best for everyone.

My limited view of the scene
and not knowing what you had in mind
(just what I'd do if I were you)
limits my perception
considerably.

I tend to pray:
"Lord, here's the problem
and here's the solution.
I'll just watch while you solve it."

Teach me to pray, Lord,
without dictating
or slipping my plans into your pocket . . .
to listen to you

hopefully and patiently
   awaiting the answer.

And show me how to handle this . . .
especially if I'm wrong!

Hooked!

She dangled the bait
and I swallowed it
hook
line
and sinker
and now look where I am!
I accepted the office
without so much as a by-your-leave
in your direction, Lord,
and now I'm stuck for a year.
Did you want me here
or had you selected someone else?

Help me, Lord,
and guard me against flattery
next time.

Fighting All the Way

Lord, I'm fighting all the way
like a fish on a hook
unwilling to be caught
resisting your leading
ignoring your voice.
Giving you my life
in one generous package
frightens me.
Why do I hold back?
What do I fear?
I almost give over
when some good Christian warns,
"But you'd better be ready
    for what's required of you!"
Her tone and expression
    imply dire consequences.

Lord, is your will always dismal?
The trials of my life were not *your* doing;
I see now I caused them myself
but from them I learned to lean on you
and trust you.
Bless those who are saved
safe and secure
once and for all . . .
and bless me,

reluctant
fearful
confused
backsliding . . .
but your child still.

Who Rang?

Was that you who called, Lord?
Did you call and find the circuits busy,
the channels jammed with my chatter?
You never send a busy signal.
No matter that 10 billion people
    are talking with you —
you still have time for me!
I'm guaranteed an instant audience
with my heavenly Father.

But when you call
you cannot say the same for me.
Often I'm voicing my needs
pleading for an answer
ignoring the still, small voice.
Let me learn the many ways
    in which you speak
and help me keep the line free.

New Year

It's a new year, Lord,
and here we are facing it together.
The old year had some rough spots
physically and emotionally
but you were with me and we made it!
Now, Lord, this beautiful collection of days
  is spread out before me
tempting
enticing
challenging
glorious
three hundred and sixty-five chances to
  show love!

Lord, I had the same chance last year
but I muffed it.
Help me this year,
this lovely, untried, unsullied year
this pristine collection of weeks and months
hours and minutes
to do *nothing without being guided by
your love*!
A large order, Lord,
but yours is a large and generous gift.
Together we can make it!